Glittery Glam

The name pretty much says it all.

Would you describe yourself as
fancy, glitzy, glamorous, fashionable
or someone's little princess?

If yes, then let the "Glam" begin.

This book gives you fun and easy ways to
add sparkle to your day using the super blingy,
super glittery scratch-off paper included.

So grab the stylus, turn the page and see how
to add some "Glittery Glam" to your life!

⇧⇧⇧⇧

What To Do:

In the back of the book you will find an envelope of glittery scratch-off sheets. Take one out and let's begin!

1 Grab the wooden stylus and sharpen it with a pencil sharpener. Use it to draw on the scratch paper to uncover the sparkling glitter below.

2 Begin by drawing things you like. Try some flowers and hearts to get you started.

3 Try making lines that are thick and thin, straight or curvy. Add patterns or a few squiggles.

4 Completely scratch off the inside of a heart to make it super, super, sparkly.

tip: Don't worry about messing up; more glitter is always better.

Fanciful Flowers

Create a beautiful flower pattern.

1 Take out a new scratch-off sheet or make your own (See P. 32).

2 Begin by drawing several big flowers that have thicker outlines.

4 Add lots of details to the flowers. This makes them sparklier. Hang your beautiful flower pattern for everyone to see.

3 Add lots of smaller flowers to fill in all the blank areas.

tip: ♥
Cut the flower pattern into strips to make super sparkly bookmarks.
(See page 20)

Posh Pinwheel

Make your day sparkle with a pinwheel of glitter.

1 Take out a new scratch off sheet or make your own (See P. 32). Turn the sheet over to the backside.

front back

2 With a ruler, mark lines from corner to corner to find the center. Draw a circle in the center using a milk jug lid.

3 Cut on the lines as shown, but be careful not to cut into the center circle.

4 Flip the sheet over and scratch a beautiful design.

5 Fold each of the tips up to the center and secure with a thumbtack into the eraser end of a pencil.

A-Door-able Tag

Welcome your friends to your room with an "ultra glamorous" door tag made by you!

1 Take out a new scratch-off sheet or make your own (See P. 32). Cut the paper in half using scissors.

2 Trace a circle at one end of the paper. using a paper towel tube or a small lid.

4 Decorate the door tag with hearts and flowers. Add a fun saying like: "The Princess is in the Room."

3 Cut out the circle by starting at the side as shown here. (this makes it easier to put the tag on the door knob.)

tip: Make a different door tag to suit your every mood.

9

PRecious Pet

Draw your dream pet... real or pretend.

1 Take out a new scratch-off sheet or make your own (See P. 32).

2 Draw an outline of your dream pet animal. Are they large or small, hairy or smooth?

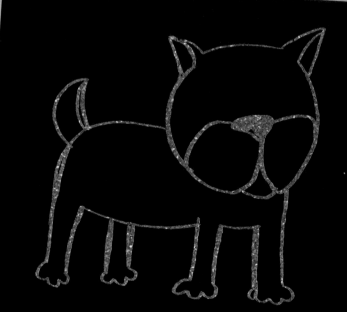

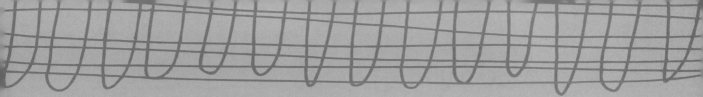

4 Glue your pet picture to a piece of colored construction paper. Cut the paper into a fun shape to make a super cute frame.

3 Now add some details. Draw some eyes, a nose, maybe a collar, or your pet's name. Show their favorite food, toys or activities.

tip: Make your frame even more special by adding glitter.

Stunning Stencils

Anything you can trace can be a stencil.
What will you use?

1 Take out a new scratch-off sheet or make your own (See P. 32). Find some cool objects and trace a few shapes on the page.

2 Fill in the areas of the shapes with different patterns.

Stencil Ideas

Cups, caps, cookie cutters, your hand, leaves, kitchen utensils, and fridge magnets. Whatever you can find.

3 Try scratching with other items like a plastic fork. Fill in the entire page for maximum sparkle.

Glitzy Greetings

Make a ritzy-glitzy card to give a friend.
Anytime is a good time to show you care.

1 Take out a new scratch-off sheet
or make your own (See P. 32).
Cut the sheet in half using scissors.

2 Fold a piece in half
and draw the outline of
a beautiful butterfly.
Make sure the wing
tops touch the folded
edge of the card.

3 Cut out the butterfly shape, being careful not to cut where the wings touch the fold.

4 Decorate the front and back of the card with cool designs. Write a special note on the inside of the card.

Try drawing a fancy cake to make a birthday card.

Fabulous Frame

Make a fancy frame to hold a favorite picture.

1 Take out a new scratch-off sheet or make your own (See P. 32). Cut the sheet into four equal pieces.

2 Place your photo onto the sheet and lightly trace around the photo.

3 Decorate the frame edge with swirls and gemstones, or hearts and flowers.

4 Use a glue stick to attach your photo to the frame.

tip: For more sparkle, add glitter glue or sticky gems to your frame.

Glam your Name

Feel like royalty—write your name in glitter.

1 Take out a new scratch-off sheet or make your own (See P. 32). Write your name in fancy. curly lettering in the center of the sheet.

♥ Use these letters as a guide.

A B C D F G H I J K L M
N O P Q R S T U V W X Y Z

2 Draw a line around your name that follows the curves of the letters. Keep drawing more and more lines until you reach the edges of the page.

3 Cut out the final shape. Use the leftover scraps to make smaller glam names for notebooks and folders.

Bejeweled Bookmarks

Make a bookmark for someone special... like yourself!

1 Take out a new scratch-off sheet or make your own (See P. 32). With a pair of scissors, cut the sheet into three equal pieces. (Try using decorative scissors to create

2 Use a hole punch to make a hole → in the top of each bookmark.

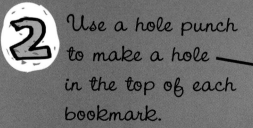

4 As a finishing touch, cut a piece of ribbon and tie it through the hole.

3 Now the fun part: drawing the cool designs on the bookmarks. Remove larger areas of black to make the bookmark super sparkly!

tip: A bookmark makes a nice gift for a friend or teacher.

Blingy Bracelets

Make a bracelet for each of your BFFs.
They are fun and easy to make.

1 Take out a new scratch-off sheet or make your own (See P. 32). Cut the sheet into eight equal strips.

2 Decorate with strips containing words, flowers, shoes, hearts, or whatever you like.

Cover the bracelet strip with a piece of clear mailing tape to protect it while you wear it.

Wrap the extra tape around to the back and trim as needed.

4 Make a hole at each end of the strip, and use a piece of ribbon to tie on your bracelet. What other jewelry could you make?

SParKLy Tiara

Feel like royalty with this fun-to-wear tiara.

1 Take out a new scratch-off sheet or make your own (See P. 32). Cut the sheet in half using scissors.

2 Draw a tiara on one of the halves, and cut it out.

3 Cut the other half into two pieces. These will be the sides of the tiara.

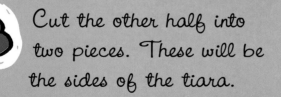
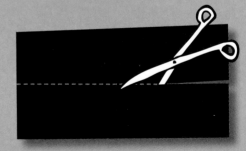

4 Flip all of the pieces over, and tape the two strips to the sides of the tiara.

5 Turn the tiara over and decorate it with gems and curvy swirls. the sparklier the better.

6 Trim the sides to fit around your head and secure with tape. Wear with pride.

CHIC CAN

Your art supplies deserve a little pampering, too.

 1 Take out a new scratch-off sheet or make your own (See P. 32). Wrap the sheet around your can and trim it to fit.

 2 Decorate the cut sheet with patterns or drawings of whatever you like. You can write your name or say what's in the can.

Pencils

create

meow

DRAW

cute

3 Make the can really sparkle by scratching off big areas of black. See the close-up below.

4 Attach the sheet to the can with glue or double-sided tape.

tip: This would be a great gift for a favorite teacher.

Sparkling Spirals & Stars

Make a glittering spiral to sparkle in your room.

1 Take out a new scratch-off sheet or make your own (See P. 32).

2 Trace a large circle onto the sheet using a bowl as a stencil. Cut out the circle with scissors. Draw little stars onto the scraps and cut them out.

4 Hang the spiral up with pretty ribbon. Use tape or glue and more ribbon to attach the stars to the spiral.

3 Decorate the circle with stars and spirals. Then, starting at the outside edge of the circle, begin cutting into the middle in a spiraling pattern.

Glittery Snowflakes

Make a flurry of glittery snowflakes.

 Take out a new scratch-off sheet or make your own (See P. 32). Scribble a pattern over the entire sheet.

 Fold the sheet in half, and then in half again.

Folds

3 Using scissors, cut out little shapes from the fold edges of the paper.

4 Unfold the sheet. Hang the sparkly snowflake up with ribbon or tape.

No two snowflakes are alike. How many different ones can you make?

Used all the paper?

Make some more of your own. It's fun and easy!

 Grab a sheet of thick paper and color it completely with markers. Make patterns, stripes, or whatever you like.

 Next, color the entire sheet of paper with black crayon.

 Now, you are ready to carefully scratch your picture using the stylus.

This book includes several sheets to get you started. Just color the following pages with black crayon and scratch away!
Have fun!